ALL ABOUT FABRIC PRINTING

Printing on fabrics has been enjoyed for centuries. Some of the earliest versions were made from carved wood blocks with dyes made from roots and minerals. Silk screening is a printing process in which ink is pushed through a screen and areas that resist the inks are embedded in it. Silk screening came from the need to automate the printing process for running yardage. Roller printing has the printing image engraved onto a tubular screen that has ink applied to it and then rolls continually over the fabric. The digital age brings all sorts of new possibilities to the world of printing with the ability to use any number of colors. The projects in this book take more of a hands-on approach, which always leads to one-of-a-kind results!

TODD OLDHAM

Designed, written and photographed by Todd Oldham Studio:
Yoshi Funatani, Greg Kozatek, Tony Longoria, Hillary Moore & Jennifer Whitney
Models: Azra, Miranda, Saevar & Samir
Library of Congress: 2012900699 ISBN: 9781934429921

AMMO
AMERICAN MODERN BOOKS

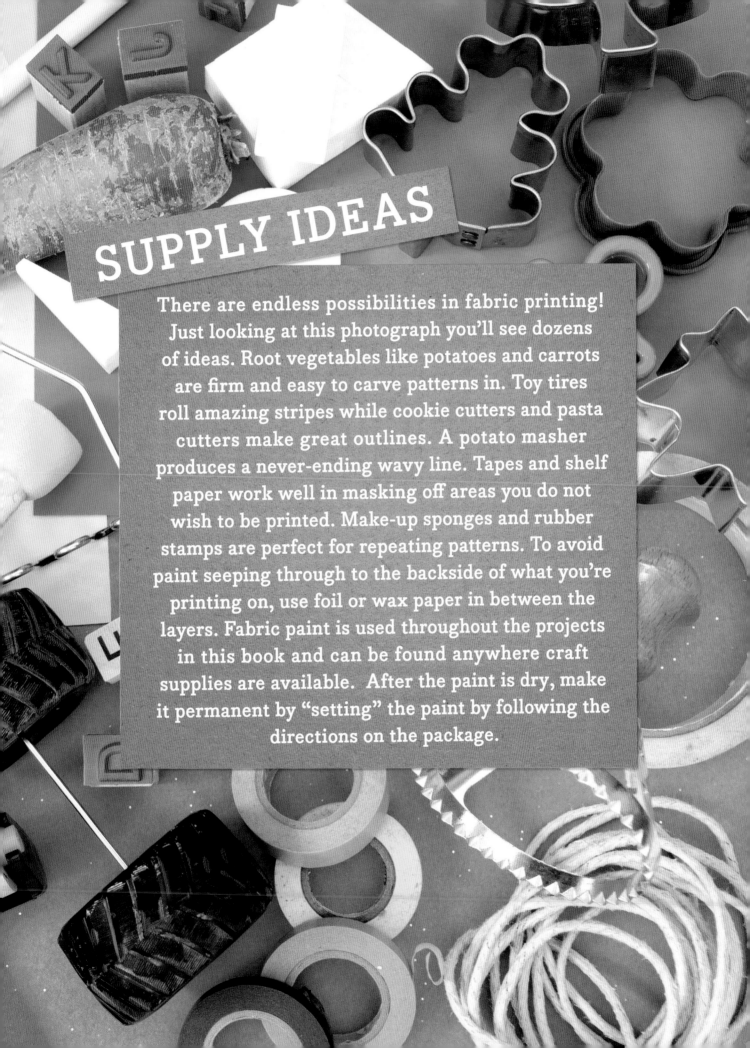

SUPPLY IDEAS

There are endless possibilities in fabric printing! Just looking at this photograph you'll see dozens of ideas. Root vegetables like potatoes and carrots are firm and easy to carve patterns in. Toy tires roll amazing stripes while cookie cutters and pasta cutters make great outlines. A potato masher produces a never-ending wavy line. Tapes and shelf paper work well in masking off areas you do not wish to be printed. Make-up sponges and rubber stamps are perfect for repeating patterns. To avoid paint seeping through to the backside of what you're printing on, use foil or wax paper in between the layers. Fabric paint is used throughout the projects in this book and can be found anywhere craft supplies are available. After the paint is dry, make it permanent by "setting" the paint by following the directions on the package.

HAPPY STAMPER

create your own custom patterns by using easy-to-find rubber stamps

SUPPLIES

YOU WILL NEED
rubber stamps (you may create your own by sending your artwork to an office supply store), washed cotton t-shirt, permanent ink stamp pad (or use fabric paint on a sponge for a stamp pad)

1 Work out your design on a piece of scrap paper before you start applying it to the t-shirt. Lightly place the stamp on the stamp pad and then place it down on your t-shirt. Press firmly on the stamp and lift away.

2 Continue applying your design around the t-shirt. Be careful not to move the stamp while on the fabric to avoid smearing.

3 When finished, let dry or "set" the fabric paint using the instructions on the bottle.

SHOE
STRING
THEORY

abstract stripes roll right
on using supplies straight
from the kitchen

YOU WILL NEED
shoestrings, washed glass bottle, fabric dye, sponge brush, washed t-shirt

1

Tape one end of the shoestring onto the bottle and wrap the shoestring flat around the bottle.

2

Secure the loose end of the shoestring with a piece of tape.

3

Apply fabric paint to the shoestring with a sponge brush. Applying one color will give a graphic look, while multi-colors will create a more painterly look.

4

Start at one side of your t-shirt and roll the bottle across.

5

Continue your pattern until you have completed your design. Re-apply fabric paint when needed. "Set" the fabric paint as instructed on the fabric paint bottle.

PATTERN OVER PRINT

make up your own
3D patterns using
make-up sponges

SUPPLIES

YOU WILL NEED
sponge brushes, fabric paint, washed printed clothing, assorted make-up sponges, paper plates

Pour a small amount of fabric paint on a paper plate and dab the sponges into it, covering the sponges' surface. You may use a sponge brush to apply the fabric paint evenly to the make-up sponge.

1

2

Place the sponge down onto the fabric and press lightly. Carefully lift away from the fabric to avoid smearing.

Complete your printing design and "set" fabric paint by following the instructions on the fabric paint bottle.

3

WORD-UP BUTTON DOWN

let your clothes do the talking with this super easy stencil technique

YOU WILL NEED
stencils, fabric paint, paper plate or
bowl, painters' tape, sponge brush

Tape down the stencil letters
to say what you want.

1

2

Carefully sponge on the fabric paint through
the stencils, being careful not to smear the
fabric paint underneath the stencil edge.

Let the fabric paint dry completely before
moving on to other parts of your stencil
design. "Set" the fabric paint by following
the instructions on the bottle.

3

HOT POTATOTE

printing with potato has never looked so tasty

YOU WILL NEED

fabric paint, paper plates or bowls, large potato, cotton tote bag washed and dried

. Cut the potato in half and place the cut end into the fabric dye. Carefully place down onto the tote and lift off the potato half.

. Repeat the printing by placing the potato next to the former print and continuing across the tote. Change colors of fabric paint on the next row.

. Continue down the tote, slightly overlapping the three printed ovals until your bag is complete.

. Let the fabric paint dry completely and "set" the fabric paint as per the instructions on the bottle.

SUPPLIES

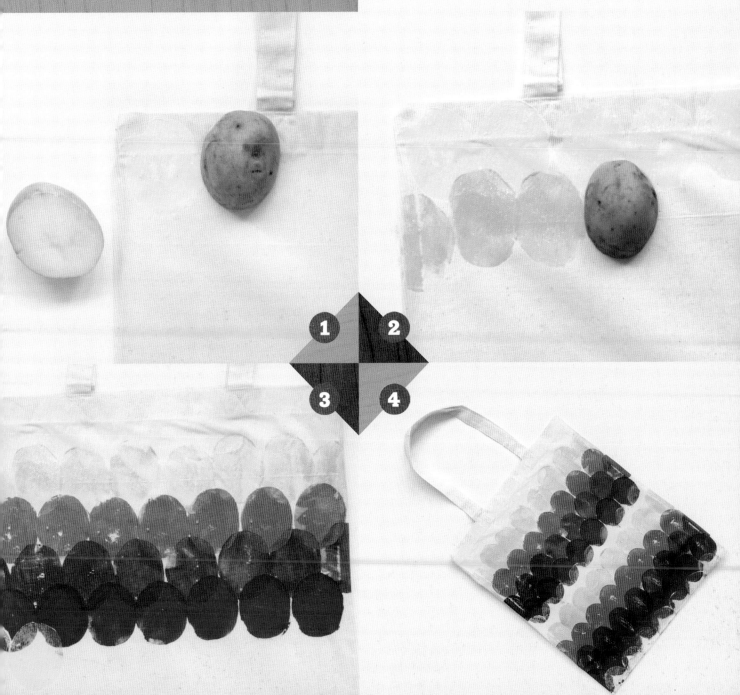

1 2
3 4

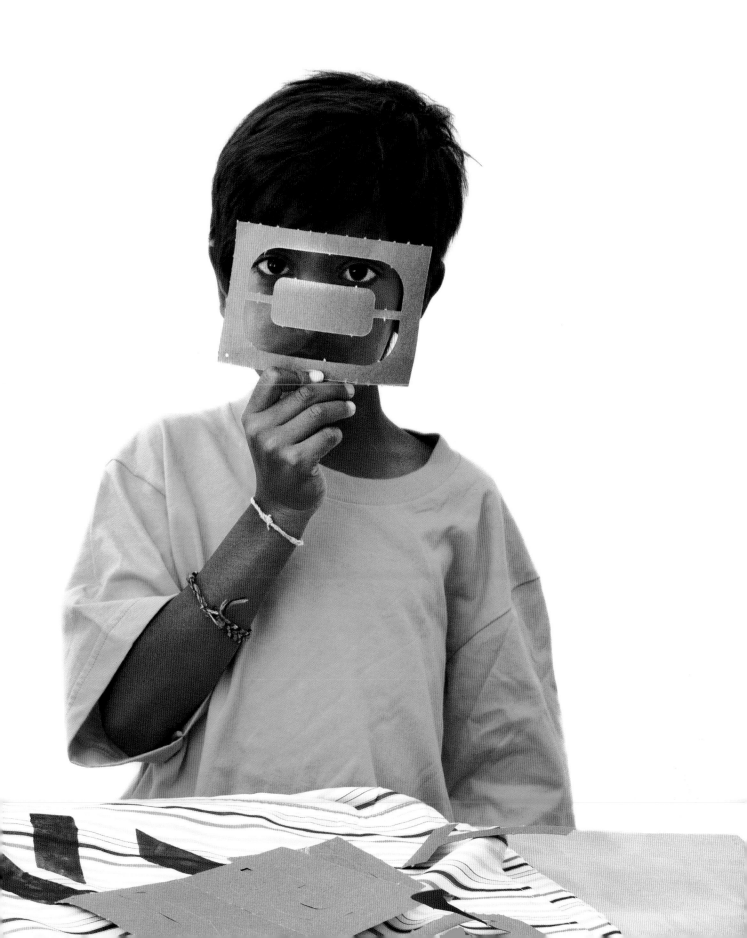

SWEATER
PRESS

chunky knitted
sweaters can make coo[l]
warm-weather design[s]

SUPPLIES

YOU WILL NEED
washed t-shirt, old chunky knit sweater, fabric paint, paper bowl, and sponge brush

1

Use the sponge brush to apply a light coating of fabric paint to the front of the sweater, making sure to cover the surface well.

2

Work quickly to apply the fabric paint to the sweater until it is completely covered.

3

Carefully place the t-shirt on top of the sweater, lining up the neckline of the t-shirt to the neckline of the sweater.

4

Use your hand to press down the t-shirt onto the sweater. Make sure you press down the entire t-shirt.

5

Carefully lift off the t-shirt, pulling it away starting at one corner. Let dry and "set" the fabric paint using the directions on the bottle. You can also make a one-of-a-kind garment by "setting" the dye on the sweater.

KITCHEN SINK ZIP-UP

cookie cutters + old toy
tires + potato mashers =
one cool hoodie

YOU WILL NEED

washed cotton hoodie, fabric paint, paper plate, cookie cutters, ravioli maker, potato masher, old toy tires

1

Smooth out the hoodie so there are no wrinkles. Pour about ⅛ inch of fabric paint into a bowl.

2

Dip a cookie cutter into the bowl, making sure the surface is completely covered. Place the cutter down on the hoodie and lift off carefully.

3

Repeat stamping until the patterns are complete. Continue printing until the front is finished and let dry.

4

...mooth out the sleeves. Pour ⅛ inch of fabric paint onto a paper plate. Roll the tires onto the plate, making sure to cover them ...pletely and then roll across the sleeve to create interesting prints.

5

Flatten out the hood and continue printing. Let dry and "set" the fabric paint by following the instructions on the bottle.

HANDS ON PRINTING

you will give this easy printing technique a round of applause

SUPPLIES

Pour a small amount of fabric paint onto the plate. Place your hand into the paint until covered and place down on the t-shirt.

1

2

Repeat the technique and continue your designs, switching colors of paint as you like.

Complete your design and let dry. "Set" the fabric paint as per the instructions on the bottle.

3

creating custom printing
shapes is as easy as
cutting out a snowflake

FANCY

FELT

PRINTS

YOU WILL NEED
paper plates, sponge brush, felt, scissors, fabric paint, washed tank top, brayer

Fold the felt in half. Fold it in half again, then make a diagonal fold to create a wedge shape.

1

2

Make an arch-shaped cut along the top, creating an ice cream-cone shape. Cut notches into the folded outside edges of the cone shape.

Cut notches along the arch side and unfold.

3

4 Trim away any rough edge.

Repeat the previous steps and create another felt snowflake.

5

6 Use the sponge brush to pull a thin layer of fabric paint across the paper plate. Lightly place the felt snowflake onto the plate, making sure the entire surface is covered in fabric paint.

7 Carefully place the snowflake where you want, making sure to not smear it on the tank top. Use a brayer or your hands on top of a paper towel to firmly press down the snowflake and lift off.

8 Repeat the printing steps on the next snowflake.

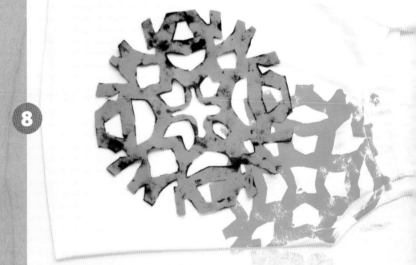

9 Repeat printing the snowflake again if you wish. "Set" the fabric paint using the instructions on the bottle.

MASKING TAPE MOSAIC

make your own mosaic pattern on anything using painters' tape